Out of a Mist that Blinds You

Poems
by
Valerie Laub
(Theo)

For Haley,
With blessings,
Theo

Valerie Laub

Copyright © 2015 Valerie Laub (Theo)

ISBN: 1515332519
ISBN-13: 978-1515332510

for Michael, my brother, my hero
for Robin and the other angels
and for Iza

Valerie Laub

Out of a Mist that Blinds You

Table of Contents

I Think, Yes
This
Quiet Day
The Things I Know
So It Is

Valerie Laub

Acknowledgements

So many people have encouraged and supported my writing. I hope you all recognize yourselves as part of this circle and, please know, I kiss your eyes and hold you in my heart.

Out of a Mist
that
Blinds You

Birthday

A golden fetus
rises from the earth,
pushing up from beneath
last year's grey, rotted leaves.

I expected to wake elated
but instead I felt alert, curious, keen.
Surely something was being born.

I waited, watched for signs:

Joy came first.
Then poetry arrived.
Then my arms opened wide.

At last, through closed eyes,
I saw the shining heart
of everything —
of those I love and those I don't;
I saw the shining heart of grass
under snow; the way birds chitter
and dive; I heard trees,
their simple song,
as they bent blue shadows
across the white earth.

Born into a cathedral of light.

The Way Birds Arrive

All that's needed
to snuggle up close
within the sweet fur of my skin,
is to welcome this day —
icy, grey, not a bird in sight —
and slip into this moment,
exactly as it is,
not asking for anything more.

Fingers fold around the pen,
nib scratching across the blank page —
magic of letters, words appearing
out of nothing, out of emptiness,

the way birds arrive
when you hold your hands
open and wide.

Barely a Splash

I love waking in the still dark,
then sitting, eyes closed,
not even waiting.

Time, if you believe in it,
passes, and suddenly the sky
behind the dark pines, is just barely light —
turquoise-blue with a sheen of yellow green
above the purple hills.

Clouds, like enchanted dolphins,
dive across this little window of infinity.

It comes to me
with barely a splash,
a knowing I have never known:
I belong.

Me, who is quirky
as they come; who
has often felt unloved —
I belong.

Not for anything I do or don't do.
Not just because I am kind or selfish
or forgetful or funny. Not just because
I keep my house somewhat clean.
But because, like you, I want a life
of meaning and passion and purpose.

A life where I wake up in the still dark,
and light grows all around me.

So now I am going to tell my secrets

First is to say
I do not know
who I am.
Simple as that.
Ignorant as a tadpole.
I barely know
how to breathe.

Second is my fear.
How every day
I walk through the world
waiting to be flung into the ether.

Third, that my life is small,
the eye of a needle,
except,
when I start to pull threads,
the tapestry that unravels
contains planets and
black holes,
dark matter
and stars.

Namaste

Who would have thought that love,
yes love, would visit me?
Oh, I don't mean a lover — at least
not anyone in particular. I mean
the way the blue day begins in darkness,
everything waiting.

The dearest things —
rising without pain,
hunger that can be satisfied,
believing the world
embraces me too.

This, I tell you,
is a miracle.

In a hidden corner of my heart,
I've discovered
tenderness; a little shy
but nevertheless courageous —
a hand willing to gesture:
"I see the beauty in you
spilling over,
the way snow
spills out of a grey sky,
softening fences,
gathering in the delicate arms
of paper birch ballerinas,
every blessed flake unique."

Something in my chest flutters with delight.

Nothing I can explain.
Just waking up.

As Of Yesterday It Is Spring

You wouldn't know it:
spitting cold
and, above bare branches,
a colourless sky.

But one little bird, invisible,
singing its heart out,
and suddenly I remember
the fragrance of hyacinths
the Spring we moved
from the prairies —
from dog dirt
and rotting snow —
to England,
world of crocuses,
and shops where the women
called me dear.

I was a child then
and it was lovely, but
now I am back
to a Spring of ice
and snow

and I love it.

I love living in a country
where the return from winter
is not easy or fast or even beautiful;
where you skitter along
on top of ice gnawed
by repeated thawing and freezing.

Persevere for yet
another few weeks;
run your tongue
along the edge
of endurance —
a minor saga of survival

while one brave bird,
singing in the poplar trees,
unfolds a new world
leaf by leaf.

Rise Like the Sun

The mountain outside my window
is so bright with sun and snow
that I can barely raise my eyes.

This morning, down by the river,
the path through the woods was ice,
rutted with yesterday's footprints
where someone had walked when the sun
was high and the day was warm and the surface
soft, malleable. Then out onto the open
shore.

It was early and the sun was low,
tangled in the branches of poplar, cottonwood.
The river ran deep blue between banks of ice.

How is it that my life is so blessed?

Last evening I watched a movie,
something true, about war and butchery.
I think how so many people suffer and suffer
and suffer. Then rise like the sun,
willing to be kind.

Standing on the shore, that's all there was.
No questions. No answers.
Just this.

Sweet Surrender

I knew I'd never
get my ice-cleats off,
my laces untangled,
the door unlocked,
and my pants down
in time.

So I did the sensible thing —
I headed to a private corner
in the backyard. I'd done it before.
No one can see and the trees
don't mind. But this was Spring
and the sun was shining and
the snow was rotten and
the path was narrow and
I slid into deep snow,
staggered, and fell
full out on my belly.

Then I rolled over,
sat up,
and peed my pants.

You might think it is hardly worth
a poem, but you may not know
how very accepting
snow can be —
no humiliating whispers
or shaming sniggers.

I was allowed to be
a guileless, unflappable woman,

just sitting in the snow
in her backyard,
laughing, as if she knew
all about love,
and the sweet pleasure
of surrender.

Northern Spring

It is difficult to work when the sky
is awash with the scribble of birds
and I must keep rushing outdoors
to gaze upward.

Every Spring this is our enchantment —
not flowers, which are cowed by cold
and who can blame them?
not green leaves, although the buds
whisper, "courage, courage,"
and puff out their little chests —
no, we have a sky etched
with prophecy and joy.

Geese honk at regular intervals,
carve long, precise V's.
Cranes scrawl an ever-changing hieroglyph,
all the while laughing and calling out, "Huzzah!"

Anyone would think migration was a lark.

All through the town people stand
staring into the limitless blue
as if they can read the future
in feathers — wings opening,
closing;
as if Spring
were as simple
as heaving the world
onto your shoulders
and dancing.

Return of the Sandhill Cranes

I wake to the sound of angels laughing.
From the warm nest of my bed
I imagine them circling the field across the river,
then swooping gracefully north.

This is Spring,
the mind's own creation.
All day the sky
has been a perfect tapestry of feathers –
a high, thin, gossamer thread
you cannot hear;
or a distant clamour you cannot see;
until, at last,
a great, gleeful cacophony –
winged gods, flinging themselves
across the clouds,
giddy with adventure.

All matter quickens
beneath the blessing of awareness —
hallowed water sings a keener song,
boulders dance across the desert sand.
Gratitude sends me reeling through the house,
passers-by all agog
at the sight of a middle-aged woman
whirling past the windows,
through the door,
out into wild open spaces.

Spring.
The dog escapes her leash.
The loon loves her lake.
Among the yellow grasses of the field –
angels laughing.

Out of a Mist that Blinds You

When first we went to the river
mist shrouded the valley.
We couldn't see a thing.
All we had was hope.

Then the world appeared —
suddenly
as a fairy-tale kingdom
revealed to the hero:

mountains gleaming with snow;
green water galloping to the sea;
a field and five horses —
white, blond, three shades of brown.

I've never been close with horses
but I've always admired the way
they light up a land,
make it real.

Today, for some reason,
I saw the horses as themselves,
long tails swaying,
their irresistible grace.

Today, for some reason,
I saw everything as itself.

The dog and I sat in the sun,
her muzzle resting on my thigh,
eyes searching mine.

I wanted to explain to her,
how sometimes,
out of a mist that blinds you,
life arrives, full force —
tree buds swollen with Spring.
And I, who have never ridden,
gallop bareback deeper and deeper
into a mysterious kingdom,
not even knowing
what I seek.

Beauty Will Save the World

When it seems
no poem
is near enough
to hear

stop

go deeply
into something
beautiful,
which can be
anything
at all.

Every soul
has its passion.

All the flower
asks of us
is presence.

Prisoner of Wonder

I like to start my days with beauty.
First I bless my eyes.
Then I bless the world.

Dawn — mist meandering among trees
that suddenly shine apple green
below the deep, deep hills;
the mountain swathed in cloud,
only its jagged, snow-streaked peak
visible in the very centre of the sky.

I walk this trail every day;
and today, once again,
it is entirely new.

Bronze sedges
bowing and swaying,
wild roses silvered with dew,
flash of wings,
raw cry of a crow.

There are days when beauty
is a thief,
all my careful plans are spirited away,
and I am left helpless, hobbled,
a prisoner of wonder.

Sweet smell of cottonwoods,
this infinite sky.

Ladybug, Ladybug

Ladybug, ladybug
fly away home,
your house is on fire,
your children will burn.

Mama, sometimes
I don't know who is me,
who is you. The way little girls
skip down the street —
fingers laced,
eyes, words, hair
all tangled.

You taught me
what you knew about love –
cruel, not to be trusted.
I showed you magic tricks –
how I could disappear,
hold my breath
forever
and ever.

So many innocent things
permeated with danger —
nursery rhymes;
a child's heart;
the way love bursts into flames.

Almost

Like a word on the tip
of the tongue, or a note
wavering on the wind —
I almost
remember the day.

I must have been six, maybe seven.
It would have been shortly after
we first went to the Rockies
and I believed the trees
greening mountain slopes
were grass, despite
what my brother told me —
the truth, for a change.

The photo shows my mother
and me. Below us, surrounded
by mountains, a lake —
large, turquoise, shaped
like a fallen angel.

We had had a picnic (something rare),
and sit in bright sunshine
among heather and sedges
with our knees almost touching.
I am wearing happiness
and a beige sweater,
wool, with red flowers woven
into the pattern. I remember
this sweater — hand-knit,
although not by my mother,
or anyone I knew. I remember
the rough feel of the wool,
and how, in my mind, it evoked

the story of a home where things
were simple, and warm, and could be trusted.

We both turn towards the camera,
my eyes closed by the brilliance;
my mother's eyes shaded
by glasses so dark
they are impenetrable.

She is almost smiling.

Nothing Left to Burn

My mother wanted her real life
just as desperately as I want mine;
to live so close to the soul that,
come death,
there is nothing left to burn.

Before the current of her life
sucked her under,
she had girl friends,
and boyfriends, and laughter.
She liked to swim in the early morning,
have picnics, walk barefoot on the beach.

Then came marriage,
a wave she couldn't crest —
gin at noon;
oblivion by nightfall.

She never swam again.

She told me that once
she had been caught
out in the boat in a storm.
When darkness fell,
her friends built a fire
on the beach
to guide her home.
I like to think of that night —
my mother, soaked to the skin,
rowing through the crashing
black waves, hair dripping in her eyes;
blind to everything
but distant flames.

Mad Dog

Edmonton.
The woods above the river.
Creeping among cottonwood, birch,
we played as if our lives
depended on it —
ready to kill or
be killed.

Once, a mad dog
chased us
through the woods.
Screaming, we were,
inches ahead of slavering jaws,
deadly teeth.

We blundered home,
knees buckling,
breath ragged.
Then your father
walked in, laughing,
his stained khaki pants
the very colour of mad dog.

Served us right,
we shouldn't be over there.

"Oh, Tom."

Our mothers,
huddled around the smoky table,
tumblers of water
the colour of gin,

said there was a madman
escaped, maybe hiding
in the woods.

We knew it —
his lunatic smell
barely masked
by the sweet scent
of cottonwood.

Ice Cave

It would have been so easy
to die there.

We entered as if compelled,
nothing to consider but blue,
blue ice.

Ceiling streaming; creek
a white rush. Ice flowed over rock,
laid its frozen cheek against the ancient earth,
shining. The walls were smooth,
sculpted. Our hands slid over the surface,
slipping into every crevice,
every crease and fold.

We had been seduced by caves before,
under the earth and black,
sat in darkness solid as stone,
and listened to the centuries:

   drip

                          drip

          drip

drip   drip

        drip

I would have listened for hours.
I would have stayed until I didn't know
if I were sitting, standing,
or dissolved.

This cave was blue.
Did I say? Blue
as bones.

I come from a cold, cold place:
Edmonton in winter;
my mother's womb.

I want to tell you.

Buried in ice,
there was a woman –
her thigh, her perfect breast,
her round belly, shining.

Perhaps there are stories
     I don't know.

We went as far as we could go.

The cave ended in a pool of water,
ice floating across its depths
like so many dragon-headed ships.
We stood on the ice-bound shore,
surrounded by light,
shining.

Badlands

I don't remember what was so funny
but you stand by the car,
wearing the coat we bought
for $2 at the Drumheller Salvation Army,
hooting with laughter. Maybe
it was because of the fog —
that trip, every morning
was a weather adventure.
Or maybe I was dancing, wearing
my 'new' hat with the ear flaps
that made me look like Elmer Fudd
on LSD.

We were friends then.
Whatever broke us
hadn't happened
yet.

I don't know what it was
any more. Something
that sculpted each of us
long before we met;
something we didn't remember
and couldn't forget.

The Badlands.
Canyons
where dinosaurs
lived
and died,
died in droves.

All the photos of that trip

show us hamming it up,
almost undone by laughter.

That day the wind was so bad
we set the camera up
then posed, clinging
to ancient rocks and each other,
both of us staring past the lens,
tears streaming.

Thief in the Caravanserai

What keeps us true,
divining rods quivering
with thirst, swaying
to find the source
of hidden water?

What wakes us in the night,
wide-eyed, petrified,
trying to decipher if this is murder,
or the shriek of some relentless bird
on the hunt?

In that great darkness,
when silence falls
and we don't know
whether we are dead
or alive,
who are we then?

When I neglect to lie down
upon the living Earth,
and pray;
when I refuse the giddy joy
of flowers bursting with faith
after unexpected rain;
when I think I can rise above
this suffering world
and not mourn with all my soul,

then I become as dry
as last year's stream bed,

desiccated as a leaf
abandoned in the desert.

I become a thief in the night,
slitting water bags
in the caravanserai.

Eagle Eyries

Once, years and years ago,
we hiked up a valley
and over a high ridge,
then skated down a slope of scree
to another world.

It may have been snowing —
tight, biting pellets;
and, even though it was summer,
a devilish wind
may have whipped our faces.

It was as if we were walking
through a mythical land.

In the second valley
there were pillars of stone
jutting suddenly upwards.

I don't remember whether or not
they were topped by eagle eyries
but in my mind they were; yes,
they were.

At the end of that valley
was another pass,
and a glacier;
and, by the time we got there,
a night sky strewn with stars.

It comes to me as a mystery,
not to be solved —
not the hike or the eyries —

but the way I am there now,
passing beneath towers
of wind-scoured rock
as a high wild shriek
crosses between worlds.

Death in the Morning

It was early, still cool,
although the sun had risen,
staining the shed with light.

I donned the vestments —
attending to zippers,
velcro, elastic cuffs,
two layers of gloves.
A veil covered my face.
I did not hurry. Every detail
was its own prayer.

I opened the shed door carefully.
Entering the way you enter
an ancient temple
where the very dust motes
say holy, holy, holy.

Two nests. Perfect.
Round. Light as air.

Imagine spending all day
under the sun,
sipping nectar;
buzzing among blossoms
of the plum tree;
craving fallen fruit.
Imagine building your home
with your teeth.

The first nest was empty.
The second began to buzz.
One wasp. Solitary. Like me.
Wanting its life.

I'd like to say I turned then and left.
I'd like to say I decided I could share the shed,
that a few stings may not be the worst thing;
that if I could never again retrieve my lawn mower
I could live with grass that grew
and grew inexhaustibly, grass
tall as trees.

I'd like to say
I chose to build
a house of grass,
joy buzzing
through every blade.

Harvey Mountain

It was a perfect day: sunny, cool breeze;
alpine flowers softly blooming — paintbrush
tinged with peach; devilish monkshood,
peering from beneath their deep cowls;
bright pink moss campion, so tiny
and so brave.

I don't know how many times
I fell to my knees
in prayer —
if astonishment is a prayer.

Little streams cradled by moss so green
it made my heart ache;
tiny waterfalls that knew nothing
about being small in the scheme of things,
and therefore weren't small at all;

pools so mysterious, so delectable, so inviting,
that I took all my clothes off
as if I had courage for frigid water.

Instead, naked, alone on the warm
rough rock at the edge of the pond,
I stood transfixed, utterly porous.
Everything entered all at once —
the sun, the sparkle, the secret whisperings
of water, air and earth;
and I was gone, nameless
as the white flowers that bowed to the breeze.

Ganokwa Basin

First of all there is the tundra –
heather and sedges and
the delicate, hardy saxifrage.
Then the velvet mosses and verdant lichens;
tiny tarns, some still with ice,
turquoise, at their center.
Creeks spilling out from cracks
in the very rock, waltzing across
the astonished green meadows.

As if that weren't a miracle.

Wind if we're lucky.
Clouds shredding the sky.
Mountains with their stony steepness,
their goats and their patches
of snow like so many piebald ponies.

At one point fog rolls in
so thick and so low
there is only the ground
beneath my feet, and your voice,
close by but invisible. We find
our way by the tilt of the land.
We know to keep the rise to our right
and not climb too high.
At the pass the fog lifts
and here we are, exactly
where we are meant to be.

How blessed we count ourselves —
not to have found our way,
but for the day:
mountain goats suddenly dashing across
the meadow, all in a flurry;

glimpse of fuzzy hatchlings,
wee nest burrowed into the ground;
the toothy marmot at the door
of his den, curious, as we are —

blessed to stand under the sparkling sun,
the buzz and hum of summer mountains
blowing through us.

A Great and Sacred Silence

The arctic sun surprised us all.
It was that warm and the water so clear,
so enticing, that we swam in the river.
Would you believe it? That far north.
The stone shore was white as bones,
sculpted smooth, silky.
I had to dance barefoot, had to,
couldn't stop myself,
my thirsty feet sliding
over the graceful earth.
Then I disappeared, breathless, into the green deep.

At night we camped where we would.
There were no stars.
And although the moon was full
we never saw it. Nights were bright as day,
sun shining in the tent.
        Even now darkness seems unaccountable.

Falcons cried out at us.
Pacific loons skimmed overhead.
Once, while setting up my tent, a caribou
ran close by me, his great rack
spread before him, an open hand,
a wing, a beacon.
I can tell you,
I did not breathe for wonder.
Another time, a grizzly sauntered
through our camp while we slept.
Everywhere we went wolves had been before us.
Their paws, big as my hand, marking the mud.
I heard them howl in the night and I dreamt
of two great black beasts with shining eyes.
Awake, I knew I was surrounded. Always.

The wind was ferocious.
We had to paddle with all our might.
Breaking camp before breakfast,
then whaling our canoes
through the endless waves,
whitecaps pitching against our bows.
But we were determined, unbeatable.
    This time.

When finally we reached the Arctic ocean
the washed rocks were shining,
black and red, black and red, black and red.
I swear, the gods play checkers on that beach.
The water, not unexpectedly, was cold. And black.
My feet streaked with it. In the distance,
ice.

During those arctic weeks
what I loved most were the low, furry hills.
When you climbed to the top, heaving
through gullies of dwarf willow,
the tundra stretched forever, bounding with peat,
soft with mosses, lichens,
each with their own smell –
this one sharp, that one buttery –
with sedges and bearberries,
their leaves already turning.
A flat land, fantastic, secretive, subtle.
Distance lost its meaning and you couldn't guess
if that was a nearby rock or a faraway muskox,
    until it moved.

Nestled among the hummocks on the tundra,
among wandering caribou and wolves,
grizzlies hidden by the gaping emptiness,
I felt entirely safe, whole,
utterly at peace.

All I need to say is there,
in that rich, desperate land,
held dear by earth and sky,
the green tongue of the river
snaking through me.

A great and sacred silence.

The Dog's Grand Passion

There is a dog, small, black,
and wet, who loves to chase
rocks in the river shallows.
(And when I say, "love,"
believe me, I mean love.)

My role in the play of this small, black dog
is to throw the rocks. Rock after rock after rock.
I throw rocks until my arm hurts and my shoulder aches.
I throw rocks until the river is choked with stones,
the beach bare, night threatens and winter bites the air.
I throw rocks as this small black dog,
careless of stars and seasons,
dashes through the rollicking waves.

Once home, I return to my passion —
seeking words that bring my day to life.
The dog, sprawled under the dying sun,
dreams of rocks flying;
the sheer glory and glint of river spray;
her sweet, sleek black body plunging
through the perfect poem of her day.

Tall

I am one who favours cold:
nothing better than snow
piled up to the roof,
a wicked wind howling
and the night huddled low.

But these days of summer —
sun tender in the morning,
steely by noon;
a breeze sibilant as water,
lifting the leaves, then
soothing them down again;
the river running turquoise
and cold, but not too cold,
not for me —
riding the current into an eddy,
blinking and sparkling,
slick as a seal.

My eyes are birds
darting with delight;
my eyes are bees
drenched in honey,
blessing all that can be seen;
and (with a wink)
all that remains invisible.

Oh, these days of summer
my long, bare feet
wrap the Earth around.
And I am tall,
so tall
I barely fit in houses.

What is the Sound a Creek Makes?

When you sit on the mossy shore
of a high-spirited creek
and all you do is listen,
what do you hear?

What do you see
but some sinuous white animal
bounding over rocks,
plunging down the sides of mountains,
brave despite the whisper of ice to come?

Open. Close. Open.
Seasons.
Wings.
The moon.

We become the world
with the part of ourselves
that is constant as stars;
fierce as fire
for the simple oxygen
of our senses;
by the holy act
of letting a creek
flow through us.

Autumn

What joy
to wake to a damp, cool, grey morning
and find, when the clouds part,
snow low upon the mountain.
To walk between the dripping trees
and catch the sharp, prickly-tart odour
of high bush cranberries. To return,
after months of cacophonous summer,
to the sweet remembrance
of silence, sitting at the desk,
aware of the tiny moments –
the silver sheen of last night's rain
on the tin roof of the shed;
the even breathing of the sleeping dog,
smelling like a wet rug after her romp.
Strewn across the table-top,
a few bright red autumn leaves.

Memory: colouring pictures of the first Thanksgiving,
the woods aglow and the turkey gobbling.

In the afternoon I stack the jars –
huckleberry jam, raspberry.
I collect windfall apples,
buy maple syrup,
stock the cupboards,
bake desserts.
Flannel sheets come out of closets
and sweaters are resurrected.
Screens come off the windows.

In the evening I will light the fire.

At dusk, in the back garden, I stand still,
and let the wind, buttery with birch leaves,

halloo right through me.
All this colour and splash,
all this unheralded leap and bound,
this gift, this grace.

I spread my arms wide.
I lift my face to the sky.
I dance.

Every Question Burning

Have you noticed
how sometimes,
for no reason at all,
the ground falls away?
You step into a room
that you have walked into
every day for years
and the breath whooshes
out of you.
Or you wake up
expecting the morning
to unfurl quite naturally,
but when your naked feet
touch the cold floor,
all you feel is cold.

I don't mean the world
is less than perfect —
birds shoot across the windswept sky,
sun slants across the valley
turning autumn trees
into pillars of light.

But I have so many questions,
every one of them burning:

How do I disappear
into this endless moment
the way my dear dog,
sweet muzzle raised to the heavens,
dissolves in ethereal bliss?

How do I
give myself to life
with anywhere near
the grace of a raven?

Never, Ever Give Up

Here's what I want to know:
Do you have to swim an ocean
to be okay? To be a success
it probably has to be the Arctic Ocean.
You probably have to swim miles
under ice, not even surfacing for air.

But what if you don't want
to swim an ocean? What if
you need to breathe? What
if giving up is simply realistic?
Means you get to survive.
Means you get to be present.
Maybe even enjoy your life.

What is failing, anyway?
I guess if the farthest shore
is the goal and you drown
mid-way, then you've failed.
But we've all heard,
"It's the journey, not the destination."
And, "As long as you try, try your best,
try your damnedest; do everything
possible, short of killing yourself."

Or maybe kill yourself, but
in pursuit of a goal,
not just because you're miserable.
That would likely be labelled failure.

So what is success?
If you don't want to swim an ocean, that is.

Could it possibly be gathering all the broken
pieces — little shards of shell, the tiny
pebbles that crippled you when they sheltered
in your shoes — could it be collecting all those
scraps and bloodied splinters and setting
them across the beach, building a mosaic —
something that includes both light and shame;
even admitting that a few chunks of the picture
may have tumbled off to the side,
are lying half-buried in sand?

Nothing glued together
except with mercy.

Have I Loved Well?

Does it count as love if you leap up
from the breakfast table and rush out,
feet bare and clothes not yet buttoned,
because the rising sun is stroking
the tender underbellies of the clouds?
Is it love enough if you creep into the golden woods
and throw yourself down beneath the naked trees,
weeping for autumn and for beauty, plain and simple?

Love may not look like two lovers entwined.
Love may have to be tapped from the solitary
gnarled tree you find rooted
at the very edge
of the wind-rocked heights
that knows only snow.
Mere survival may require clinging to Earth
without the aid of gravity.

So how do you love well?
First, you write your own language, poetry
that cracks you open, offers you up —
a willing sacrifice. Then,
maybe after the snow flies, burying you
beneath its selfless and vital silence, then,
if the Earth turns and the ground thaws and
Spring arrives, all green and shining, maybe then
you can rise, twigs in your hair,
leaves in your teeth,
and claim love with words
that are your own,
and true.

Origami Morning

Out of darkness
light wraps itself
into wings.

Pine needles,
birch boughs.
Stark lines
etched black.

Clouds
suspended,
serene.
Soon
they will burst
into flame,
set the mountain
ablaze.

A neighbour's light flickers on.
Small sparrow flashes past.
Fallen leaves, frost on grass.

Why should this,
just this,
bring such exquisite joy?

My heart
flying.

Odaray Glacier: Final Climb

Icicles hang over your head.
You are wearing crampons,
clinging to the ice.
Dark glasses reflect snow,
sky — edge of the world.
Rope joins you
to some invisible other.

Turquoise trousers, purple fleece,
red harness, blue rope.
I like the colours and the ice
and the sun and how I can read
both triumph and exhaustion in your face.

It is one of my favourite photographs
of you: my brother, my childhood hero.

Now, you tell me that your breath
is shallow, your lungs constricted
by the tumour that is your liver.
There are tests, doctors,
clinical trials.

After you came down
you said it would be your last big climb.

You couldn't have known then.

You tell me the larches have turned,
already well past their prime.

Every Day I Wonder

Every day
I wonder whether God exists –
as if I don't believe
the rough bark of pine trees,
the sudden sting of sleet.
As if my words were bird bones;
my life a stillborn child.

Listen, heart.
Listen to the tender ache of hope,
the bruised pulse of fear.

Tear open the frail fabric
of this flesh,
we find a universe of stars
and empty spaces.

This is who we are.

Seeds burrow into the earth.
Ravens fling themselves
into the ether
with perfect faith.
Longing curls inward,
soft paws dreaming.

Every day
the blue world
remembers itself.

Singing Underground

My sister-in-law tells me
that the oncologist
turned to her and my brother —
who has liver cancer and laments
that the avalanche hazard is high this year,
limiting back-country skiing —
she turned to them and asked
how it is that they are coping so well
and what should she tell
other couples who come
with cancer galloping through
their marriage, cell by cell?

The answer was lost
in my own tears
but had something to do
with how my brother faces things
in a very pragmatic,
intellectual way.

At which point
I reminded my sister-in-law
about the stained glass window —
huge, heavy —
that my brother and I
climbed ladders to install
(upside-down)
in their living room and
how, in that instance, my brother
wasn't all that intellectually inclined
in how he expressed himself.

And then we laughed.

All day my heart ached with love —
all day and all night;
and still I hold a precious gem
that is like sunlight streaming
through birch trees
sprouting golden leaves
among their naked roots,
as silver-winged birds dart,
singing,
underground.

Once I Saw Horses

Look at this rain-soaked day:
a near silence; loneliness.

How to see a rain drop
clinging to a leaf,
and not imagine falling?

Once I saw horses as themselves.

They stood motionless,
yet the earth trembled.

Christmas Cactus

I stand in the doorway, breathless.
How did such a miracle happen?
While I was sleeping, no less!

Pink birds.
Fuchsia.

They started off as tiny feathers.
No, they started off as nothing at all.

Then,
one morning...

wings unfurl, fly from the stem,
beaks outstretched, yellow tongues
licking the air, raucous cries
irrepressible.

How could I have slept through it?

All of life is like this:
Plant a seed so small
you can barely feel it between
your rough, gnarly fingers
and, come summer,
it feeds you for a week;
as you wash dishes,
leaves turn into snowflakes;
a mountain rises
by moonlight.

Then, one morning,
blossoms beat extravagant wings.
Something soft and tender and shining

opens in your breast
and everything, everything,
is inexplicable,
is blessed,
is holy.

Swan Song

First snow.
Just enough to whiten the roofs;
frost the crackling, golden leaves;
line delicate limbs and tender twigs.

Along the narrow trail
the dog acts as if she smells
a bear and I clap my hands, if not
for safety, then for wonder.

A single cry.
I look up — bare branches
scrape the sky —
swans!
O swans!

You know they are swans because
against the sky they shine white; because,
unlike Canada geese, who gabble
and yammer the whole way south,
swans are largely silent.
You know they must be swans because
you feel your neck elongate, your heart lift,
you feel yourself rise above the earth,
feathers extended,
tippy toes barely touching.

Swans!
O swans!

When you see them,
if you have a song,
you are singing.

I Wanted to Stand There Forever

The sky was pale green.

The river, which two days past
had been flowing free,
now twisted a line of liquorice black
between banks of blue ice.

A wan sun, veined with trees,
lay down upon the waters.
Small bergs bobbed downstream.

Below me, where the river turned
toward the distant sea,
I could hear a slurring, sighing,
stuttering susurration
as the ice slowed,
merged,
welded berg to berg.

I wanted to stand there forever.

Everything flowing
and shifting
and then
stopping.

Yet under the surface
water swirled and,
every moment
ice was transforming.

Tomorrow
great shards will heave skywards,
frozen turquoise,

roaring.

Jesus Saves

I've taken to wearing
my brother's cast off long johns,
top pulled low over the crotch.
I may look eccentric but I don't mind
as long as I am not compared to the man
who jogs around town, hour after hour,
with shorts over his long johns
and JESUS SAVES
scrawled across his t-shirt.

These seem like jolly long johns,
and perfectly decent.
They go well with my sparkly red hat;
and they suit the songs I sing
voce piena as I swing along the streets.
Nor do they impede the dance steps
I practise on the trails.

They remind me
of gliding down the long road,
my first winter on skis,
when my pack fell forward
and thrust me head-first
into suffocatingly
soft snow.

My beloved brother pulled me out,
both of us almost dying with laughter.

Now? Now? Now?

I wake early. It is not yet dawn.
I creep to my desk to write –
a poem, about snowshoeing
across the flank of the mountain,
the Arctic sheen of the windblown crust,
sun dogs embracing the fickle sun –
but the dog has heard me, is awake
and in the kitchen,
toe nails tap-dancing across the floor.

"It's too early," I say.
She leaps and pants.
"It's still dark," I say.
Her tail thumps against
the cupboard doors.
"I want to write," I say.
She whirls with delight.

Who can deny such enthusiasm?
Who can resist such unfettered eagerness,
such anticipation of joy?

I open the door and she hurtles outside
to wait
while I pull on my boots,
        my jacket,
                my hat,
                        my scarf,
                                my mitts;
then close the door behind me.
She leaps all four feet high into the air,
        "Now? Now? Now?"
                Now.

No stars.
Mountain and poem both lost in clouds.
I stump along trying to think of clever phrases,
scintillating metaphors;
but secretly thrilling to this poem,
this lovely, wintry, not-yet-dawn romp;
my sweet dog stopping to grin back at me,
her old eyes glinting
as she draws me towards the light.

Snow

I can't help it;
I love it when it snows.
Even though it is difficult
for the homeless, the elderly, the ill,
I love it.

I love the sky falling in tiny
torn promises, every one unique.
Some are just a word, others a phrase,
and when they settle all together
they lay poems on trees
and hedges and fences and roads.
Poems settle on dogs and people
and eyelashes and, if you look up
and stick out your tongue, you can swallow
a poem, just like that.

I love to ski through the woods,
poems floating past the pines,
and match my breath
to the timeless cadence of snow.

I disappear
and all that's left is snow,
is poetry, is this perfect world.

Last Winter

Snow like silk. Ice crystals
nipping the air. It was cold,
oh yes, it was cold.
Sun glimmering between
trees so thick with snow
I could barely keep
from doing a sprightly
ski-tip pirouette.
As it was I took the curves
on one leg, arms flailing,
blinded by laughter
and tears,
my eyes watering,
for you.

This winter you rarely get outdoors,
a trip to the hospital
now and then.
I wonder — do you miss
the icy air, the low slant of light,
star-swayed nights?

I learned to ski with you.
In fact, I learned
almost everything with you.

That first winter,
you'd haul me out of snowdrifts,
set me upright, and away we'd go,
grinning through chapped lips,
squinting through the ice
that lined our eyelashes.

I've learned to stand alone.
Almost alone. You are there,

as you are everywhere.
In a way, I'll never be alone again.
Always the sun will be just behind
the snow-laden spruce trees.
Always my heart will ache with love.
Always laughter will be laced with tears.

Winter Demands So Much

Winter demands so much of us.
I don't mean the cold, and the thick,
bundling clothes; or stumbling
through snowdrifts on lumpen feet;
or the way the wind
slices across your face
as you creep down paths
of alarming ice.
And I don't mean
the eternal, shuddering nights.

No, I mean the light,
how it calls to us, demanding
we attend to everything,
and all at once.

The back yard, for instance.

Most seasons you can go about your day
and ignore the yard; not have breath
sucked from your lungs by a glimpse
of poplar shadows wavering blue across
sun shot gold. You can move from room to room
without suddenly being halted by a glance
at the hedge, so pillowy and softly sculpted
that you yearn to sleep, just there, where the snow
is tucked under, clean and kind
and utterly inviting.

Most seasons you can move through your life —
east, west, mountain, moon —

turning away just before
splendour
brings you to your knees,
and everything
you once knew
is lost.

Swarm of Light

You are going soon.
No longer able to eat,
to stay awake;
skinny arms and legs —
vines, winding around
the seed of your death.

Oh we will miss you!
we will miss you the way fire
misses oxygen.

All about you there is light;
an incandescent blizzard of love —
snowflakes wetting the faces
of your wife, your daughter,
your sisters, your friends.

You.

This is what surprises me —
that in my mind,
you have joined the circle
of your own death watch.

You stand there, wide awake,
legs roped with varicose veins,
(you are wearing shorts, of course,
and hiking boots) and
despite the driving snow,
you are grinning.

Something Infinite

In the night
I dreamt that cold
speared my soul
and wouldn't melt.

I knew, the way one knows
frost has trampled the flowers,
that it was because
I had abandoned poetry.

Poetry is not words;
it is bearing something
infinite in your heart
as you creep across
a crackling pond
towards an uncertain centre.

Ice starts at the periphery,
a pattern of petals
and crinkling leaves.
Tap a toe
and a thousand fronds shiver.

It is not solid ice
I seek; it is a love
so fine it defies gravity.

<u>here, in my heart</u>

winter.
such a dull day.
snow spitting past the pines.

somewhere,
not far away,
my brother is dying.

my sister-in-law says
he would like to see me,
but wouldn't want me to see him.

I do see him — his humour —
that time skiing down the road
we stopped to climb to the top
of tree stumps, then
tumbled into the drifts below, free-fall;
the way he has always accepted
my formidable eccentricities;
my poetry; me.

oh, I see him.
I've seen him for years —
a man of such integrity
it makes my heart weep with pride.

whether I am there
or not, I am there.
I kiss his eyes
and hold him in my heart.

the day is grey, snowflakes
winnowing down from the sky.
I hear whispering
as they fall past pines,

settle on my hair, lips, tongue.
when I look up
snowflakes kiss my eyes.

there is nothing left unsaid.

Beyond Blessing

All day the sky
has been a staunch,
simple blue.

Now,
air
the colour of awe.

It is twilight,

the hour of mercy
when we dare
to acknowledge
that we are nothing more
than the thrum of raven wings
skimming between the veils,

when the unblinking black eye
of infinite space
permeates every cell.

Our shivering lives
slant across a deepening sky,
like wings,
like stars,
like a prayer
known
only by its silence.

Line of Light

I woke before dawn.
All through the still darkness
I thought of the life
flowing through my body
until I was nothing more
than a column of light.

When the sun rose,
it rose like a peach.
There was fresh snow,
everything clean and white.

I skied in silence; alone,
if you don't count the trees
and the sky and the snow,
and the ravens sailing overhead.
In the new snow skiing was slow,
time to watch sunlight flickering
among the thick branches,
soft and gentled.

Now the sky has turned pale,
colourless. The sun has sunk low
behind the mountain —
but not so low that the clouds
aren't still quietly shining,
that the spindrift blowing from the ridge
isn't lit from below.

Along the roof of the shed
there is a line of reflected light

that makes my heart ache
with love for this very moment.

It is clear, crackling cold.
In the valley the river is icing over,
its dark eye closing.
There will be stars tonight.

Raven-Hearted Skiers

I love a grey sky.
Steely white flakes
swirling past dark pines,
wind clawing at my hair,
snow pecking my lips.
The strange metallic call
of ravens.

Today, the crust beneath
the new snow is smooth,
thick. We ski across fields,
sail over buried fences,
sweep down blind slopes,
the light so flat you can't see
if you are flying to heaven or earth.
We spread our wings
and call, whooping back and forth,
two ravens frisking on the breeze,
wing-tip to wing-tip,
dipping and diving,
swooping upside-down.

Below us a coyote
trots over an ice-bound lake.
Earlier, two foxes darted
through the trees —
red arrows.

I watch for wolves
but find only footprints,
disappearing.

Mama

Lately I have been concerned
with things sharp
and cold:
windblown ice at forty below;
the searing brilliance of sun on snow;
touch of metal shredding the tongue;
your love.

You were my goddess.
Glamorous. Terrible.

You wore your glasses dark,
pointed — the fashion
of the day.

To prevent snow blindness
the Inuit carved masks of bone,
narrow slits for eyes.

You painted your nails
blood-red. And your lips —
teeth streaked scarlet.

They ate their meat raw,
bloody. They didn't have metal
until we came, wielding knives.

On Not Going Skiing

It would be a perfect day —
a little fresh snow, some sun.

But what I want is stillness,
silence; to let my mind
glide through the early slant
of pale yellow light, blue clouds.

My own kitchen — cupboards that need painting;
tea towels that hang from hooks, orderly, but limp;
kettle; pot of soup. In the cold, numinous light
everything slows down, freezes into a question.

A memory I've forgotten —
something young that pulls me out of myself
and strands me, yearning.

I can almost taste it.

Outside my window
the mountain is almost lost in a fog of ice.

I wander the house, every room haunted
by white light, every ceiling raised high.

It is this that holds me here,
this almost-recollection of an ancient timelessness
I knew as a child and that winter
offers up again and again.
A holy question I cannot answer,
cannot name.

How to Manage a Moose

Last night
a moose found its way
past the high hedge
with the narrow gate
that opens into my yard.

The dog took to barking.
I leapt out of bed.

The moose was browsing
on the frozen branches of my apple tree.
I stood at my bedroom window
and waved my arms.
I threw tennis balls
but this moose had no interest
in tennis — not on this winter night
with the crusty snow up to its thighs.
Instead this moose turned
to my young birch tree with its fine
delicate limbs. I love that tree.

I went outside.
I called, "Shoo!"

The moose munched on,
pointedly ignoring me.
Insulted, I blew through my lips.
The moose, truly alarmed by a woman
in penguin-patterned fleece pajamas
and a down jacket, standing in a wintry yard
making farting sounds under a starry sky,

snapped to attention, laid back its ears
and dashed through the gate.

So there.

I may be getting older
but I can still manage a young moose.

Winter Fool

Lately,
I have given myself over
to cross-country skiing. Oh,
there are other things
I could do, but snow does
not descend as feathers,
trees are not festooned with joy,
the earth not laid with silk,
every day.

One day it will rain.
One day I will be too old,
or injured, or my knees
will give out. I am already
way over the hill and down
the other side.

But still skiing.

I like to pretend that I am an athlete,
that were I to pass anyone,
they would be brought to a standstill
by the sight of my amazing technique,
my stunning strength and speed.

(I try to be out of sight
when flailing up hills).

Afterwards I come home
red in the face, heart
still beating wildly with joy.
I am tired. I am hungry.
I am useless but happy.

I think:
It is not so much what we do

but that we love whatever it is;
that our passions make our lives
a prayer of gratitude,
a prayer of praise.

Thank you, thank you, hallelujah, thank you.

The Terrible Warmth of Snow

Mama, winter reminds me of you –
air sharp as broken glass;
the awful ache of flesh, frozen,
coming back to life;
the way you can never trust
river ice; the long,
lonely night, so dark,
and so desolate.

I choose the coldest days,
never tell anyone
where I am going.
I leave tracks, of course,
broken branches.

No one ever follows.

The simplest mistake
means death,
and the earth
steely until Spring.

I picture myself,
back against a tree,
disappearing
into the strange,
familiar
warmth of snow.

Whiteout

I like it cold,
a keen, perilous edge:
threat of frostbite;
avalanche; a blizzard
in the offing. Life or death —
and you can recognize
the difference.

My mother lived in a perpetual thaw,
snow sliding off the roof,
roads a mess of slush and mud.
She dissolved her days
watching soaps, drinking gin.

It's not what she wanted.
She wanted to be out there
on the barren plains, crawling
on her hands and knees,
saving her soul.

It takes determination
to breathe in a blizzard.
Sometimes, to survive,
you need to know why.

Drowning

Here we have a day when the world
is quiet. Even the dog is snoring
softly. This room is warm
with light. The sun is gentle,
and the sky. Snow folds itself
into blue shadows.
Crows sail past
in silence.

Part of me wonders
if sitting here,
watching the day,
is life?

But when I stop questioning,
the sky becomes an ocean
and I am floating.

Everything is timeless —
the cloud that rests on the horizon;
the light on the snow of a distant roof.

Everything is complete —
the bare alder branches;
the little bird darting in and out
of her hidden nest;
my fingers, unfolding.

More than complete —
everything, every living thing,
which is everything,
is vibrant.

They say that when you drown
your whole life flashes before your eyes.

I tell you,
I am drowning
and my whole life
is right here,
right now.

Smallest Moments

It is afternoon.
Snow blows across the mountain.
The dog, her white muzzle swinging low,
walks slowly. A prayer of presence.
Not to be rushed.

I take a step, another step.
I turn. I wait. Sun pale
through a field of grey.
She trots along,
white paws cherishing the earth.
In places the snow has melted:
yellow grass, rusted leaves.
Eyes half-closed
she stops, sniffs, trots on.
I take a step, another step,
I turn, walk backwards,
watch the wind ruffle her fur.

Dear old dog, every day
a blessing before you go.
Small moments, simple gifts:
your brown eyes, cloudy and kind;
how brave you are in snow;
the eager way you greet a treat;
that you snore – the very tip
of your pink tongue peeping out,
sweet as a poem; gentle yips
as you gallop through your dreams.

One step,
another step.

After the Dog

Cold.
Frost flowers the window.
Twilight touches the mountain.
The sky – so very blue
at noon, now pales to yellow.
The world stands frozen.
Only smoke rises – thick, woodsy,
ecstatic.

In the house, no snoring;
no yips or pedalling paws.
Age has ended
her sweet dreams.
Silence
fills the space
she left behind.

Her name meant 'love'.
I was surely smitten –
her wise, brown eyes,
tongue, so pink,
rich, warm fur;
how trusting she was,
and how gentle.
Her holy eagerness
for walks, for treats,
to have her ears rubbed.

Her holy eagerness
for
everything.

I Think, Yes

I think, how would it be
to feel your roots entwined
with another's, the way
limbs tangle in love-making.
I think, is this the very thing
I am missing
when my life feels
empty, a paper wasps' nest
in a winter wind?

I think, yes; and I think,
I must not think of it
because
this is how it is
and knowing it is true
could break my heart.

And I think
how my heart
is already broken
and there is nothing
to do, except love
all the little shards,
and jagged
hopeless
shimmers.

This

I'd like to tell you about winter,
about snow:
not just any snow — not
wet snow or crusty snow
or snow pocked with dog dirt and grime;
but this snow that is light as a breath,
deep as a soul.

This snow shimmers in the air —
a veil. You step through it,
snow kissing your eyes,
your lips, your cheeks, crystals
of ice lacing your hair, and there you are —
caught in the enchanted web of winter

(cobalt mornings,
sudden snap and crunch of cold
when you open the door,
streak of warm kitchen-yellow
spilling from windows).

In the quilted silence
the fog-wrapped moon
exhales cold.

A mountain appears —
this mountain,
indigo in the early morning;
later, a fierce, keen-edged white.

How does one survive
such beauty? You'd think
the heart would burst
with astonishment; lungs
would soar into the ether,
balloons of unbridled joy.

At twilight clouds rise above the ridge,
wings shot gold by a sun
now vanished, leaving behind
this snow, this miracle

this.

Quiet Day

You could not mistake
this sky for summer —
gentled as it is
by a high haze
of winter clouds.
Muted sunlight illuminates
the frost flowers
on my window,
their intricate,
delicate,
exuberant design.

All day, poetry
has shimmered about me —
ice crystals
in the Arctic air.
I've longed for such stillness,
nothing but light;
to watch the day,
but not from a distance —
to watch the day
as if I am the light
spilling across the white fields,
wrapping itself around blue shadows,
softening edges
until everything is hushed
and wondering.

It is so easy to get pulled away,
drawn towards the world,
and never touch that place
where we disappear
and become ourselves;
so easy to suppose
what we do is who we are:

I am a being who studies light,
bathes in the suns low, pale rays,
listens to silence as if it is a song

and I know the words
and am singing.

The Things I Know

At sixty you expect some wisdom,
life experience, knowledge at the very least —
how to roast a chicken; drive a car;
the capital of Venezuela.

The things I know
are hard to name.

I know what it is like
to have stepped over
the edge of the cliff
and stalled there,
afraid to look down

but then I do

and then I know
what it is like hurtling
through unbridled air

landing with a thud
the way one does from a dream.

Suddenly
I am in my body,
and what used to be
is now broken
and open.

Sixty.
Once I bought a chicken but
I became vegetarian.
Once I had a licence to drive but
I was a menace and gave it up.

So now I walk around all day,
smiling,
not knowing

except
Lima, I believe.

So It Is

The day was warm as April.
In February! Sun on snow,
the surface glazed. Every ridge
and cornice etched as if with acid,
shadows that sharp.

Now, a film of cloud —
the mountain steps back,
disappearing.

So it is with things we love —
winter; mountains; each other.

We start from a shining so clear
it hurts the eyes; then, things soften,
sky and mountains merge. We barely
recognize ourselves, our dreams.
One day, we realize that our passions
are substantial as a mountain, potent as a cloud.
Distance, even death, cannot disturb our loving.

Behind the ridge the twilight sky is pale yellow.
Who knows what darkness will bring?

Made in the USA
Charleston, SC
30 August 2015